L'OmBard

LiT FROM BELOW

Three Series of Poetry

Lit From Below
Three Series of Poetry

©2023 Golden Apple Publications
ISBN 979-8-9860801-2-3

Cover/Book Design: Mark Gelotte www.markgelotte.com

Printed in the United States

TABLE OF CONTENTS

LIT FROM BELOW

Lit From Below © 2020

Poems I write since age 15 come from patterns within
To connect with the patterns outside
In my 60's I find that I've now lost my leash
There's nothing about me to hide.

My deepest belief is that humans are one
With Creator and each other - God's will
So, nothing I say should really shock or dismay
The words come with only hope to fulfill.

What guides my process is light and love
And being present for others in life
And sharing oceans of lessons from those for whom I have cared
As a teacher, nurse, neighbor, and wife.

It was at age seven started on stage with the dance
That is when ideas and art started to flow
Quick understanding of life viewed as definition and lines
When bodies are lit with violet light from below.

Life meaning inspired by anatomy and bones
And beauty and skin of all hues
From dance with no words to poems now inspired
By dancing images that give me my cues.

Some artists will take on society at risk
And comment in movement or words
So please take what I say or just let it go
If you feel my risks are best seed for the birds.

I'm lit from below though no longer on stage
Others' actions give me permission to teach
Was called from my God and infused with the rhyme
With a cadence set to heal community breach.

Some words in fact heal, at least that is my hope
But knowing I cannot control is the key
These offerings simply record just a few thoughts
And feelings about things that I see.

Take them or leave them, these ditties are real
For my truth expects nothing in return,
But one thing that I ask in America today
Is give me freedom to speak not to burn.

Poetry is best read by this poet I think
So as to adapt for those who will listen to cause
Experiencing life as definition and lines lit from below
Done with rhyme and cadence so the mind takes a pause.

Thank my ancestors now who inspire every word
Irish and Scottish bones carry the genes
The gift of the gab or maybe fili
Each day reveals new poetry it seems.

Living through the pandemic as a nurse was just enough
But then the violence and hate words did not cease
They're not everywhere but a call for balance seemed right
That the poetry started to flow to bring peace.

Peace comes at a price Mohawk elder told me twice
As she passed me her tribe's story to hold
Five arrows of Hiawatha and the Peacemaker's plan
For a time when hatemongers were bold.

A brand new mind carried to a new life
Stronger in unity was the vision way back
Can't see what is in the mind but now actions speak loud
Demonstrating care and intentions we lack.

My poetry is written to honor great ones
Who have figured the way of peace and progress out
So we'll all be lit from below with greater definition and lines
Transmutation by violet is what these words are about.

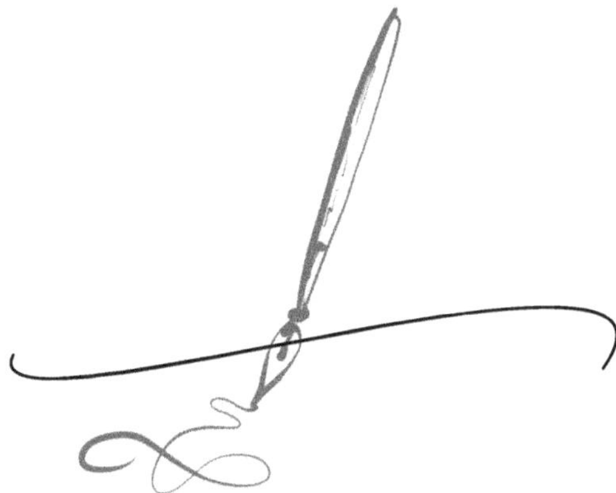

TUSHITA LIGHT SERIES

A Plum or Fig for Life

I would eat only a plum or a fig
For my stomach and spirit are full
The valley below stretches wide and
green as far as my eyes can see
Its peace and beauty fill me so.

God you have given us heaven on earth
Yet there are so many who do not
yet have eyes to see nor ears to hear
the fruit trees weighed down with their bounties
or the rustling of the leaves in the gentle breezes
coursing the valley from high to low.

Your arms are the mountains that hold the valley in form and light
And in my ecstasy, I am one with you and the valley
breathing in and out
the abundant gifts of life.

Where will we be tomorrow?
How many will turn to the valley within and above
to eat a sweet plum or fig precipitated in love and light?

I will feast each day on simple fruits
and ecstatic visions...
And with the sound of the AUM I am transported home
Once again where there are no limits on the sweetness of fruits
or the expression of beauty, power, and peace
as we know comes from the gift within.

Déjà vu © 2020

Have you seen them in your dreams?
And now they're in your space
Time – Reality – Significance – Life
Capturing memory is the base.

First and last are intertwined
May seem that we're in a knot
Tangled within and tangled with others without
Deeper meaning can actually be sought.

Some feel it's a dream
Coming forward as true
Others describe this phenom
As coming out of the blue.

Whatever the science
The impact the same
Moves a person to wonder
If they really know life's game.

Creator reminds us
There is more to explore
Mind, body, spirit are essentials
Now we know there is more.

Sparks of connection
Stardust makes a trail
The dream world now manifest
Experience lives to tell the tale.

What will you share?
And how do you tell?
Say "that's another déjà vu"
Confirming you already know this moment well.

Premonition as opportunity
Déjà vu confirming God
A guiding force that comforts
When on earth we feel a bit odd.

Connection with the eternal
Is like swimming with the stream
Join with those who explore latent powers of self
Peace of mind is more than you've ever dreamed.

Cosmic Law is Not © 2020

Not written on page nor in the stars
That which compels and commands us to beauty, kindness, and peace
Find cosmic law in spaces between the pages and between the stars.

Not easily heard though known in the stillness of the heart
Lub dub - pause - lub dub
Where do we learn right and wrong?

Not forgotten are the values written on stone tablets,
parchment, and pages
So many sages struggled to form
Memories have become ancient wisdom.

Not only simple civility - call it human rights
Or cosmic law for cosmic right
Be right in line with life, support life.

Not confused or bemused
Souls living spun of God's truth
Cells formed from cosmic dust drawn from between
the pages and the stars.

Not likely they remember much
Those who steal and loot and riot and rage
Fists raised at whom or what
Cosmic law is not demanded.

Not their way or the highway
All considered one under cosmic law
Peace rules the spaces between pages and stars
None can disrupt with force of selfish desire to control.

Not argued in a court of men
Nor in mediations leading to settlements without peers
Cosmic law backs every contract, currency, and code
Enter this courtroom with curiosity and care.

Not witnessed but known
Not sworn but carried
Written on the inside of every living cell
Codes of DNA matching peaceful protest and progress.

Not human but divine
Not yours and not mine
Cosmic law is the test
Not at rioter's behest.

Not alone – We are one.
Not a liar who is "done"
Cosmic law rules every day
Alpha to Omega is God's way.

Drops of Truth – Minds, Hearts, and Hands © 2020

From thin and rarified air
Delicate crystals forming to a point
As stalactites and stalagmites
Water and earth form on bridges and in caves
Minds await drops of true inspiration.

Ether is and is not
Here, there, and everywhere
Catch a dream of objects not yet descended
Make them a reality
Hearts await drops of true reformation.

Star dust trails of silver and gold
Sun and moon meet
At the center of cosmos creates
New Matter called words
Hands await drops of true expression.

Crystals and reality and words
Now manifest in all and for all
A gift to be treasured
New life merging minds, hearts, and hands
Humanity awaits those who carry drops of truth.

Meadow of the Mind © 2022

Climbing to the top of closest mountain
Eyes stretch to the far horizon
This place prepared by God so long ago
Seen now from highest simple perch.

Between the peaks of longtime landscape
There is delight in nature's beauty
A stretch of space for horizontal orientation
Filled in with so many soft green grasses.

Venture down and forward boldly
To the place and space 'tween peaks
The peaceful plain laid down here for us
Take several breaths and deep repose.

Amongst the leaves of grass so tender
Grow the simplest of rare treasures
Wildflowers small and red like starfires
Never to be plucked and disconnected.

Touch these beauties and the grasses
Lay your head and body down
Peace fills every cell with spirit
Everlasting memories carried in the meadow of the mind.

Out of Body ©2022

Soaring spirit
Blessed body
Stripped of earthly weight.

Flute vibration
Pulling upward
Responsibilities abate.

Oneness rising
Images blending
Freedom never too late.

Not so quickly
Treasures earthly
Gravity over rate.

First the symbols
Peaceful knowing
Fusing love and hate.

Prayer wheel spinning
Destiny earthbound
Heaven must now wait.

The Residue of Rest ©2020

Sun and peace stream through
The windows and the blinds
Open the shutters for all to see,
and feel and believe.

There are none so blind
As those who will not see
Beauty of the early morning
Opportunities to create.

Breathe deeply in the residue of rest
Between night and day - sleep and wake
Moments of choice for those who love
To fill a day with meaning and delight
Extending rest as deep knowing and peace in every act.

Tushita ©2020

Thornless rose
Peaceful beauty like poetry
Standing Tall
Across the valley for all to see.

Oh the cologne
Freedom to grow
No fear of harvest
Moon or no moon.

She peppers the landscape
Red and white
No two flowers the same
God's space forever untouched.

Her fragrance beckons
Come to me
And know a peace not far away
But carried always within the memory.

Between heaven and earth
Spaces wide the lay lines
Mother nature's divide
Birthing souls ready to serve.

Descending and ascending
For those with eyes and ears
No more thorns and no more tears
Roses and memories of Tushita

CORONA LIGHT SERIES

Consider Mother Teresa ©2020

The building momentum of danger and din
No mask or thoughts of protection
Now deemed mortal sin.

Some able to rise above self so to serve
In times of great need
As humanity's faith takes a curve.

As fear trumps good sense and control rules the day
I remember Mother Teresa
And wonder what would she say?

Mother entered every home with confidence and grace
Knowing the gift of God's presence
Would fill each and every space.

No gloves, scrubs, or masks as she tended each soul
In today's virus-dominant world
I wonder if police and governors would roll.

Would she be thrown in the clink for exemplifying her trust?
Would Mother Teresa be found guilty
For doing a soul's work she must?

Where is the line and the space anymore
For those thinking about health and well-being
A spirit they just can't ignore.

Can people act in good faith when caring for those in great need
Entering a home filled with love
Hope for healing to seed.

Where is the line for MD's would prescribe
Wear masks now forever
Even when you imbibe!

Resist the temptation a God ye would be
Who knows every virus
Has the cells' master key.

We can't study all variables though we know quite a few
Just do not forget
These viruses are lifeforms like you.

They have their own way of getting through on this earth
They've been inside and around us
Since we first came to birth.

Now consider Mother Teresa and what if she'd not
Given selfless service to people
Left by society to rot.

Some thought her an exemplar of what to become
When fears acknowledged and mastered
Ultimate destiny of some.

COVID pandemic behavior threatens faith and good will
Challenges balance and meaning
And in some spirit is killed

I venture a guess we might be surprised
Should Mother Teresa walk in
Without a disguise.

Welcome her spirit right now as we need her true fire
Move on fear of death
Replaced by joy that won't tire.

Miracle Pathways ©2020

Through the walls of towering waters
Moses let all the people free
Today we deal with COVID 19
A miracle many just cannot see.

Yet I know it is a true blessing
Some say it's now in disguise
But when we look back on our own history
We'll see it's when we really got wise.

Wisdom is earned and not given
A formula of effort and time
It's a gift so often discarded
As not being worth even a dime.

Pair wisdom and freedom and miracles
Precious values I'd take any day
The blessing of living history in the making
God-given purpose we earn as we pay.

Pick It Up! (A Messy Poem) © 2022

In 1986 I became a nurse
What once was a blessing
Now I think may be a curse.

The only mandates we had as nurses licensed state by state
Have all been winnowed into one federal mandate
"Masks for all and forever" our fate.

May I show you now
what I learned from nurses of old…
When and how to mask - a science I believed in
And a heath care culture on which I was sold?

We masked for airborne exposures
And droplets floating here and there
But we masked inside - never outside
In the freedom of the open - we were never ever scared.

We masked when around others
With diseases supposedly easy to catch
With gowns and gloves and sometimes goggles
The choices of safety around the disease always matched.

Now mask mandates indiscriminate
no idea how to teach nursing students today
The practices of the people
Unsupported by science in many ways.

But there is one thing makes no sense at all
And that's the masks I see all around
Instead of discarded after each and every use
So many now lying out on the ground!

We never would dream of dropping
A mask and leaving it there
Especially one that's used and "dirty"
A public health risk not demonstrating care.

So, if everyone is so very expert now
On infection control and pandemics and such
Still fearful of airborne diseases like COVID-19
Why would picking up a mask be too much?

Let's follow that fear for a moment
And the concerns of amateurs and experts for real
If those masks are contaminated with the deadliest of all
A dirty mask left on the ground's a big deal!

Blue paper or black and multi-coloured cloths
These masks are not graded for cure
Coronaviruses spread like RSV and some others
Despite nurses' best efforts for sure.

So this old nurse reminds "Please don't litter"
But especially with a symbol of fear now run amuck
Do your part and be aware when you drop a mask
Please pick it up - A mask wearer's karma you can't duck.

Unmasked © 2020

Some cover their mouth
Some cover their eyes
Some cover their whole face
To form a disguise.

Whatever the placement
Whatever the plan
Wear a Mask – Yes a Mask
Whenever you can!

Conceal words soft spoken
No expression or sign
The Self communicated
Now has boundary lines

What is to become
Of communication and trust?
All faces All races
Facial Covering a must.

What will now become
Of deep care and connections
Take away facial recognition
Used from birth deserves mention.

How can we unmask
For loved ones or Self
When social labels and ignorance
Threaten our very health?

Now masks give permission
To hide anger and hate
Who corrects this? Not communities
Waiting for this power to abate.

There's a solution so simple
As old as the hills
Unmask when you can dear ones
In Spirit of good will.

Be clear about one thing
Do not step over lines
Many retreat far away
As have others throughout time.

Seek seclusion in cloister
Without mask - without fear
Follow the way of the Elders
Bringing peace ever near.

Weighing benefit and risk
Between seclusion or mask
Continue seclusion with loved ones
Some will choose this task.

If heart pains continue
As panic prevails
We seek solitude in Spirit
Our unmasked God never fails.

HEALING LIGHT SERIES

Forgotten Elements of Climate Change ©2019

These politicians are oh so wrong
They speak and sound just like a bunch of ding-a-dongs
Their proclamations are so strong
Demanding that we sound the gong

What is the problem you should ask?
They say we must take on their task
To change the climate here and now
Some even have it in for cows!

But listen closely if you will
Their statements just don't fit the bill
'Cause if we're talkin' climate change
There has to be a bit more range.

Climate is not over there
Climate is not just laid bare
Climate is oh so much more
So I write this poem to settle the score.

Climate is within without
Climate change is what life's about
Elements of Self and more
Fire, Air, Water, Earth at its core.

We *are* climate can't you see?
We are its elements you and me
Being that change begins within
Don't follow politicians, they aren't your kin.

What we change about our Self
Will affect our very health
It will change Earth Mother too
If we all would think it through.

Choices we make for food and fun
And just whether to buy a gun
Would we race cars on a counter clockwise track
If we knew that it could break our backs?

Stop and think 'bout what they mean
Some scientists say doesn't mount to a hill of beans
Let's get real and work the Elements five
Forget the rhetoric - Transform the give.

Embrace yourself as climate and be
4 Basic Elements and Ether - no additional fee
The climate change rooted oh so deep
Ancient wisdom says we know in our sleep.

Waking or resting on self we gaze
Forget the "me" time, that was other days.
That Self (big S) is the platform for change
It's one we control – this gift fills the bowl.

We are the elements – yes all five
And vessels of light you will come to see
Explore your elements of Self first and foremost
And climate change you will be!

Compounding © 2020

First one element
And then another
They make good things
For you and your brother.

These pharmacists
Working behind closed doors
Compounding the elements
For products that sore.

Their costs are sky high
Not sure work they will
Prescribed by another
Who's collecting the bill.

A long history now
Of passing the cost
To millions of souls
Without skills that they've lost.

They tell a true story
We cannot commit
The millions of dollars or euros
To make a medicine a hit.

There is a known formula
For compounding today
Keep sales numbers and effect
Equal importance they say.

So far from the roots
Of ancestral designs
Are simple herb recipes
Have healed millions just fine.

Time records us the craft
The pattern is there
For those who remember
The truth now laid bare.

Tis not witchcraft nor hopeless
To garden or play
In one's own kitchen laboratory
Makes best medicine some say.

Compounding at home
Is fun and has meaning
Making medicine with plant partners
For those with that leaning.

First flowers and leaves
Making extracts and teas
Blessing Mother Nature for plants
And our pollinators the bees.

Then digging roots for symbols
Take only the need
Teachers tell us these are precious
Medicines grown from a seed.

So please forgive us, don't hurt us
If kitchen compounding we will
And grow our own medicine
family cabinets to fill.

We know that these work
Our ancestors told us they do
We also want pharmaceutical compounds
Able to try something new.

Herbal simples and drugs
Are just not the same
Neither plants or chemical actions
Should anyone blame.

Takes a number of elements
For a really good compound
Sometimes years, sometimes tears
Producing remedies that are sound.

Pharmacists and drug companies
Seek magic bullets and cures
But the way compounds work
Requires personalization for sure.

When medicine mass produced
Without a person's pattern in mind
The outcome "hit or miss"
May be all that one finds.

There is a solution
For big problems and small
A country compounding plan
So, no one's interest must fall.

The elements of this country compound
Are simple and straight
As long as compounders and users
Check any feelings of greed or hate.

Design a country compound
A kind remedy plan
Invite pharmacy and kitchen herbals
Cultural expressions from every clan.

Why not a country compound plan
That welcomes old and the new?
Promote action and self-care
All forms of evidence our cue.

This compounding formula
For social and personal success
Is medicine-making at all levels
For our children, that is best.

Antidote Mass Consciousness © 2020

Many thoughts are not our own
They float in from near and from far
Those thoughts that cannot represent us
Or even attain our own bar.

These thoughts, they do come and go enmasse
They float in like the wind
But we can pick and choose you know
Any ideas we'd prefer to rescind.

Mass consciousness is anti-life
It resists the mind of God
Don't engage the habits to think its way of fear
Risk being the one who's called out as "odd."

God-Creator- Allah, by any great name
Wants us to think with Him
He'd never take back our gift of free will
Turning back human history on a whim.

Courage and heart at the root of free will
Effort and will fuel us to think
Let the mass' thoughts about life and all else
Keep moving on by less we sink.

The weight of these thoughts that are not our own
Would keep us in bed day to day
But we trust in our God and the gift of our souls
That we really have something to say.

Let no other human put our thoughts in a box
Instead be in the circle with elders who say,
"Speak to your own real calling and stay close to your truth"
Then watch free speech and free will win the day.

Adored Priority © 2020

Scientists know not the mind of God
So why do they speak so firm?
As if they know everything about the universe
From people to climate to germs.

They do not know and that's ok
We respect scientists all the same
As long as they do not cross over the line
And take over our way of playing life's game.

God's on the throne inspiring thoughts and free will
And we are his children on earth
Nothing scientists have done or ever will do
Can rival the ecstasy of witnessing childbirth.

Truth be told I too am a scientist at heart
Pulling patterns into an organized view
But knowing my place in God's eternal plan
Is my first priority from which I take my cues.

There is a line between arrogance
And the place where we enter in
God - please dance with us and take the lead
With trust in you we always win.

Beyond © 2021

Reach out into the space at your fingertips
Then extend further – stretch beyond

Cast your vision to the front door of your house
Then crossed the threshold- walk beyond

Drive your car to the end of your town
Then accelerate at the green light - go beyond

Remember your life as it has been to this day
Then live another day- breathe beyond

Teach your children to love their brothers and sisters
Then send them to school- engage beyond

Eat a pizza and enjoy the tomato sauce
Then try to grow your own tomatoes and make your own sauce -
respect beyond

Go to the bed side of an elder passing from this life
Then stay as they exhale one last time- experience beyond

Sit very still and focus on your body head to toe
Then imagine life without your precious instrument- gratitude beyond

Take everything near and far into your thoughts
Then open your heart to all creatures great and small and those that
you might have forgot - open to the beyond

Imagine heaven on earth where all is beauty and form and vibration
Then take the first step to manifesting it- be the beyond.

Blessings from Babies © 2021

There is motion everywhere
I see faces move then they sing
Hands move then they clap

There is fragrance all around
The dog runs by and his coat is wet
Mother has just washed her hair

There are new tastes every day
Taking in milk and water
Then a fruit or grain grace my lips

There are sounds of life I am learning
People who know me say my name
Some sounds are too much for me and
I wish again for the womb

But if you will invite me to stay
And if you will remember the challenges of transition
to this world

Maybe I will be more comfortable in my body, mind, and soul
And in that peace recall each exquisite blessing I have
brought here from
our God.

Can't Stop Creativity © 2020

Ideas like lightning bolts
Fill Your head
Then flashes of color
Or perhaps objects instead.

The process unknown
Though beautiful indeed
We know not the brain
That we will concede.

But probabilities aside
And possibilities a must
Gather these ideas like lightning
Before power makes one bust.

Can't stop creativity
It's power is a fire
Expression of Self
A flame that won't tire.

The purpose could be
To build the ego or "I"
True creative flashes are often
A surprise to the receiver – Oh my!

What should one do
When standing under a waterfall?
The single solitary person
Can't stop the flow at all.

Beauty and process unknown
Received by one and not all
Records a gift of Creator
Rather than an ego with gall.

Society must bless
The creatives in their midst
Especially the children
Well – you get my gist.

Fear stifles the gift
Of flashes of beauty from above
Don't dam up the waterfall
Of the descent of God's love.

Create a place for creatives
And the heart will expand
Solutions to tough problems
Are so close at hand.

Reach out to creatives
And give them a hand
Include them in meetings
Before you get in a jam.

Creatives bring waterfalls
Ideas, beauty, and such
They might spin your head
And your heart strings so much.

Can't stop creativity
Though that's how some spend their time
They even stifle the flame within
Jung analysis - they're just mimed.

Let's all talk creativity
When social problems pile on
For humanity as a whole race
Seeking violence be gone.

Creativity suggests
A new day, a bright dawn
Opportunity awaits
Spaces and places now calm.

Can't stop creativity
Jamming and damming causes pain
As cancer or nuclear war
And even children insane.

The doctors old notion
Of one cause and one cure
Is the most heinous of solutions
Moves against creativity for sure.

How can communities channel
Creativity from one and from all
Invite flashes of color and objects
Leaders - put forth the call!

Welcome power from the unknown
Creative answers to pain
Prepare to bathe in the waterfalls
Creative process is only your gain.

EnPointe © 2020

Knowing how the pirouette is enpointe
and the hair so tight in a bun
she can twirl and she can jump
Ah, but too tightly wound she does not dance.

Holds the barre but not too tightly
Lift the chin but not too high
She can tendu and she can releve
Ah, but too tightly bound she does not dance.

Sweet Jesus fill her heart and soul with praise
And her arms rise to greet the Creator, sun and moon
She can arabesque and she can ronde jambe
Ah, but too tightly ground she does not dance.

The music transports her
beyond time and space and lyric
She can plie and she can fouetté
Ah, but too tightly found she does not dance.

Then one day she discovers the music and praise now internal
She lets go of the barre altogether
The tendus and plies become effortless
Ah, but she is loosed, and messy hair goes where it will ...
She dances to the sound within that rises to
meet the morning light.

Entering the Circle of Respect © 2021

We glean respect
And it is seen.
We earn respect
And it is learned.
We demonstrate respect
And it is created.

The path of respect is a circle
gathering travelers sometimes weary
Seemingly no end in sight.

Where does this path lead?
Some skeptics ask who do not know
The power of the circle
And it's energy sublime.

One voice emerges from the circle
A gift to others is ordained
To speak of secrets lost millennia ago
And recovered in victory today here below.

Momentum is gained in constancy
Focused direction round and round
Never failing to praise God for the glory
For each test at a new cycle sounds.

All bodies start to hum
As warp and woof the circle does spin
How many join is beyond human thought
They even dance on the head of a pin.

All are tested for a quotient of faith
Lifetimes of beauty and a measure of heart
Those who find they're not ready or willing to spin
spiral out pretty much right from the start.

Going back to the world to manifest greater respect
For the Creator and all self-made men
Focus on joining those who are willing to learn
Of galaxies from beginning to end.

There are souls and evolutions who know only respect
They teach from the heart it is true
And when dis-respect becomes the rule of the day
They emerge from the circle on cue.

Defending the faith and the victories so earned
Drawing those pure in heart to the circle of God
It is easy and seamless for those who are ready
While others think the circle just odd.

As the Self-made one joins all others
And the momentum accelerates in tone
The circle of community of persons respecting all
Gains wisdom that we are never alone.

The circle of oneness springs now without fail
Light bursts out from each and every heart
A new dimension then forms, a pattern emerges
The spiral of respect is now playing its part.

Remember the role that one person can play
In seeing, learning, and creating respect in life
A vision appears at the end of each day
The circles now spiral beyond strife.

Eternal Memories of Delight –
A Poetic Endnote © 2019

Lay a strong <u>base</u> for the collection of my memories,
your memories, our memories

Design a welcoming <u>space</u> where inspiration from
above and treasures from below meet

Fill the floors, the walls, and ceilings with gratitude and <u>grace</u>

Create a <u>place</u> to bring the gifts and do the work
Set the <u>pace</u> - the rhythm where you will retreat
from the world each night

Bring out your favorite <u>vase - showcase</u> your favorite beauties
planted outside as colorful greeters,

Base – Space – Grace – Place – Pace – Vase - Showcase
I have won my race!   Imagine the smile on my face?

No need to mourn for me...
I left this house, my home on earth
Directly for my heavenly home
My place of peace and rest.

Charlie the cat has returned to my side,
He waves his tail and I my hand,
As memories saturating this space - this place
Are washed by rains deep into earth's soil.

Warmed by the sun, drawn up to the sky
Forming clouds in which you will see are etched
Patterns of my eternal memories of delight!

Friendship of an Angel © 2020
(Inspired by the Archangels Gabriel and Hope)

It is love that attracts these beings of light
When not directed to them they must stay out of sight.

They work with us to make clear every scene
Of human love wisdom and power - their senses so keen.

They guide and guard and make way when they can
But only through love, can they help any man.

Now invite them with words, they're waiting with wings
Flapping gently on air to make our hearts sing.

When the world disappoints during this long dark night
Remember to speak loving words to your friends the Angels
who would bring you their light!

Greed © 2020

Arms so wide
Never satisfied
Trinkets glow
Only focus - here below.

Taking this and that
Getting oh so fat
More and more is "mine"
Erasing boundary lines.

Endless need for stuff
Spirit is only fluff
Materialism run amuck
Happiness? Ha – Good luck.

This is the vibe of greed
Hollowness and empty need
No connection with a plan
Drive and desire to get all you can.

Divine direction from deep within
In a world of greed – maybe just a sin
Greed is a momentum of "get and grab"
How can the greedy let go of their flab?

The beauty of nature is a place to start
The solution is deep gratitude from the heart
Stop and breathe, offer others your treasures
Give of self every day - receive abundant light without measure.

Insanity at Crosswalks ©2020

In life we're all being tested
From below and above
To see if our reactions
Are rooted in love.

In my short life
Of just 60 years
Never thought something so simple
Could bring me so close to tears.

It's happened to me now
Not once but twice
That upon entering a crosswalk
Seems I gave permission for drivers to take my life.

They get behind the wheel
Only God Knows why
Their vengeance and anger
That someone must die.

The rage that they feel
Bubbles up and about
Their car now a weapon
Of their intention, no doubt.

Who is their target?
Someone walking for fun?
A woman, a person
Loving nature bar none?

The first time deliberate
Used his car to take me out
Raised his fist black power symbol
I jumped out of the way wondering what that's about.

Didn't know him from Adam
No one watching but God saw
The Angels protected me
when this human violated crosswalk law.

The second time yesterday
with my westies in tow
she seemed far away
so we entered the crosswalk down low.

The car sped up fast
as she entered the hill
she rolled down her window said "I'm sorry"
Her intention was not to kill.

Both of these episodes
Within the course of four weeks
Brings me to question the sanity
Of anyone crossing the street.

We could get rid of those crosswalks
As their purpose seems now nil
When those filled with rage or momentary blindness
They're used to find victims to kill.

The world's upside down right now
When you can't even cross
A street in your neighborhood
Without fear of great loss

So I'll write my poems
To shed some light
And to move through this time
some call the "dark night."

My soul is intact
bearing the light never fails
I *will* walk across crosswalks
Knowing God's and human laws will prevail.

Matriarch's Beacon - A Poetic Endnote © 2021

Foundation laid in friends and family
The base of the pyramid for life
She births the next generation
And serves the family circle as wife.

Growing and rearing and praying for children
She is known as the one called the mother
How is it she does what she does
So many gifts and skills like no other.

Taught me to clean my room
A skill I still value today
Keeping house and home in order
Next to godliness so many still say.

Stood by the stove when I started
The recipes I loved to cook
No matter to her the dinners were mine
And she would be soon off the hook.

Then there were the traditions like lemon bread
She created her vision and plan
A recipe she dubbed early as "secret"
Representing well the Canadian side of her clan.

The other part of her being was Celtic
from Cornwall and Channel Islands on the map
And of Irish stock too, though that too was a secret
Till one daughter historian filled in that gap.

Another tradition sounds silly but true
She said with maple syrup "never waste a drop"
She thought that was the one and only time
We should use our tongues on a plate like a mop.

She walked us to the White Mountains
On a mission, checkerberries to find
Cutting the precious berry into fours, we each had a taste
Of a flavor like no other kind.

Mom - mother - mommy - or Ma
From you we did learn many things
When to safely taste Mother Nature's gifts
And from the womb you taught us to sing.

Geography you instilled in us and your students
We always knew about our place on earth
Though you wanted us "out of your hair" on most days
Your matriarchal beacon was intact yes from birth.

Thank you for birthing and loving and teaching us
Some lessons may be too hard to share
But now as you take your flight into the arms of our God
We bless you for all of your loving care.

Your beacon intact and instilled in our souls
Life, beauty, and memories that heal
We close this chapter of our lives with much gratitude
And say farewell to Connie, the Leo life now sealed.

Momfeather's Flight – A Poetic Endnote ©2017

Straight words of a mom
Catch straightness of a feather
You're a God-free being now
And have broken the earthly tether.

Warm zephyrs through your head feather
Your beads sway in the breeze
As you walk among the elders
Your being now at ease.

As thin as a feather
Though you once took up space
We remember your poetry
We remember your face.

Delightfully free
Amazingly light
A body once burdened
Now freed from the fight.

You've won oh so many
To your vision of peace
In the rainbow bridge story
Discrimination will cease.

We're all of the rainbow
You told me once or twice
Focusing on difference, you said
Was more than a vice.

Now free to inspire
To teach from above
Take flight our dear Mother
With our gratitude and love.

My Man in the Morning © 2020

My man in the morning
Eyes soft and pink faced
Struggles of aging from yesterday
All memory erased.

Simple movement with stiffness
Deep sleep now is past
Getting gears into motion
Takes a bit longer than last.

Put a smile on your face
Realize words not a clue
Hearing and sight are diminishing
For new perceptions new hues.

Adding days, weeks, and years
To life lived to the full
Be authentic in talents
What you can't do no bull.

Time is of the essence
So they say – it is just
Bring happiness and peace
Each day, yes you must!

Sit on your own throne
Be not frightened or tamed
The finishing years of one's life
Victory's angels will frame.

My man in the morning
Get up when you will
Smile first as you greet us
All discomfort to still.

Invite us to your world
Of simplicity and grace
We long to be too
Eyes soft and pink faced.

My Person Within ©2017

The stillness within swells
As I wait for the outer attack
My person within stands ready
As the hatred mounts and fine tunes it's edge.

There are those who seek strife
As some cannot imagine
My person within stands ready
As their energy surrounds me like gum and soot.

More than one, more than two
More than three times violent
My person within stands ready
As the fierce winds blow and the tumultuous rains soak my skin.

They derange the elements and
torment
The peace of our soulful life
My person within stands ready
As I witness to the power of human suffering.

And then the sun streams across the fields
Clovers and sunflowers and grasses aplenty
My person within stands ready
For the freedom and release that enters my world
when God's favor replaces this human nonsense.

They have no power though they exert their free will
My person within stands ready
To testify as to their choices to disrupt and steal
A blazing light spurned long ago and never again to be debased.

New Growth ©2019

What is your topsoil?
How hard is the dirt?
What is your pattern?
What is your worth?

Waiting for rain?
Cups of emotional softness
Wet the cracks and barriers
Make way for seeds of potential.

Uncurling life
Shoots of green and white
Breaking through earth's density
Empowered by air and fire.

Reach out for the sun today
Tomorrow and forever
Patterns of new growth endure
Once internalized and inspired.

Ode to the Tall Grass © 2020

The brown crown lays a dormant
At the window I will wait
For signs of life as green shoot pleases
Without regard to date.

Your fronds were oh so lovely
Yet brown they were in fall
And winter snow did grace your stems
Til the time to cut did call.

We cut you down so gently
As to prompt and gently nudge
Prayers now every morning
Knowing only Mother Nature can judge.

Some say to "wait, it's only May
And spring has just begun
But I write this poem and sing my songs
In hopes that your shoots start to run.

Plea of a Pattern Scientist ©2020

To think is to dare
So important to care
Line by line the story is told
Some experience as a bit old.

While life is highs and lows
And some lives full of more blows
The measurement of purity of heart
Is often taken from the start.

Roger that to our teacher and friend
Whose timely message would now send
To those who try to catch
Inner and outer patterns that do match.

Drawing upon history and self-review
Comments on country may be new
For some blessed to be at rest
Waking now to the blessed test.

A teacher calls us to think and dare
And prepares each one to care
Examine patterns if you will
Even elements of others that could kill.

What is the test in this call?
Apply eight principle patterns to all
Preserve life, liberty, and peace
Interior - exterior wars to cease.

Cool the heat and warm the cold
Ancient wisdom works and is easily sold
Drain excess and give deficiency a boost
Build the yin and a place for the yang to roost.

No energy on planet earth left out
From pattern analysis - that's what the test is about
The call of the teacher - train minds to think
Needed now more than ever when global health is on the brink.

Please Putter ©2020

Putter,
No more plan
Pacing room to room inspired
Gentle thoughts like simple sparks
Ignite a day meant for rest in action.

Putter, Putter
No more demands
Pause to give senses a chance
Ideas break through demands of others
Stop and smell the roses blooming all around.

Putter, putter, putter,
No more willing and wishing
Practice moving like a gentle wind
Touching objects, making connections
Accessing sweet memories.

Putter, putter, putter, putter
No interruptions with your plans and demands
Join in and place yourself on the shelf
Enjoy the deeply pleasing act of puttering.

The Privilege of Poetry © 2020

Writing poetry is a privilege
Musing in the morning
Food in the fridge
Warm house, clean sheets.

Time and space to think on things
Catching ideas
The beauty of butterflies
Considered.

Fleeting moments of peace
Billow into word
Now scribbled on pages
Clean and white.

No technology yet
Thoughts stream unimpeded
Word paintings on ether
Catching vibrancy of life.

Writing poetry is a privilege
Yes, pen and ink and paper and pauses
Crafted in ideas
And words and thoughts.

Weigh the price of creativity
No one knows the risk of attainment
Benefits of hope and compassion
Coursing lifetimes, privilege pays the piper.

Rhyme or No Rhyme ©2020

Expecting a rhyme
Now she turns on a dime
My way in my head
Is sometimes better left unsaid.

Creator knows best
Divine Mother's behest
Is why I now speak
And then give it a tweak.

The words are not mine
Nor is the beauty of rhyme
Inspired from above
Descend spirit's dove.

I once thought I could
Or maybe that I should
Step away from word sounds
Dancing instead knows no bounds.

Once again, I was caught
In battle we are taught
Not to wrestle with the flow
Else we suffer a blow.

So, whether in rhythm or in prose
The poems flow as God knows
From this pen and this heart
Each day a fresh start.

Expressions of life
And sometimes of strife
Words of peace and of hope
Serving others I hope.

Surrounded by change
Over the top and really strange
Connect with nature and rhyme away
Builds more harmony throughout the day.

It is possible, it is real
To use words to actually heal
A planet of people in distress
Visions of caring are just best.

Patterns of rhyme and prose come
Hope they create peace and laughter for some
The outcome uncertain as most things all right
Thanks for listening to some poetry, please have a good night.

Simple Lesson from Orchid © 2020

Elevated flowers of delicate orchids
Green leaves provide the base
Roots peak out from the surface
There is soil, but just a trace.

Because of this we're careful
Beautiful flowers to be preserved
Watering just the very right amount
Gives lasting pleasure and calms the nerves.

How does one know how much is too much
Water with ice cubes seems the best plan
But when a flower withers all of a sudden one day
Jump into action to save the orchid life if you can.

Talk to us orchid or how will we know
More ice cubes, or water, or light
Can't lose another flower two have gone in the trash
Stick to our plan with hope you'll be beautiful and bright.

One flower now hangs in the balance
Six others still up and open wide
Breathing a sigh of relief, she seems to say all's ok
Simple lesson from orchids growing inside.

Preserving plant beauty can be a simple task
Other times a mystery for sure
No words to guide just connection with the plants
On this human life does endure.

The Spirit of Nursing ©1998

Messenger of beauty
Sentinel of peace
Service rendered from the heart
Dissonance to cease.

Gentle touching, listening
Healing presence, grace
Science mind, creative spirit
Harmony of time and space.

Understanding and compassionate
Inspiring all to "be"
Ever lis'ning to souls saying
"I need freedom to be me."

Shining winged caduceus
Joyous flight unto the sun
Enlightened health and healing
Victory is won.

The Transfer © 2021

The transfer begins
Gazing into your eyes mirroring broken body and pain
Yet fleeting as the Divine radiation breaks through
And the bliss of the memory of your mission fills us both.

We connect soul to soul
Though I cannot truly know the pain you endure
And as I feel the love in my heart expand and glow
It is beyond me to stay anchored to this earth.

Reaching up towards your feet
To touch you one last time before you leave
A shining red drop of blood from your forehead
Leaves the thorn above your eyebrow landing in my open palm.

How does one explain the ecstasy of the transfer of the light
in a drop of your blood
Filling my body in an instant and moving into the
earth below my feet
Raising plants and soil and all creatures
walking with the essence of renewal
Even before you have passed and risen again, my Lord.

The memory has never faded
The love and glory etched in my palm and heart and feet
as if it were yesterday
The meaning has only intensified as the
purpose in the transfer becomes clear
And my senses are nourished from beyond this world of illusions.

You are the conduit for one and all
Yet some have received your physical blood and
carry the memory of your life on this earth
None will ever explain the cellular change affecting not only that life
But the next and all others.

I am the witness to a transfer offered and received
Initiated in human suffering and accepted with total love
abandoning all senses and mortality.

The cross, the blood, your life for mine
Breathing peace knowing that the transfer is complete
...by God's grace...
And we move on to live within the glory of the memory.

They Come to Us © 2020

When we call
They come to us
When we fall
They reach down and lift us up
When we panic
They comfort us
When we become engulfed by nonsense
They show us reason.

When we cannot find a way
They lay a path

Not THE path but A path
As choices do remain
Try their path set before
Teachers of old and of new
Only good, only best
Vision yes, ego now at rest.

When we forget
They inspire a dream
When we are confused
They separate us from the crowd
When we yearn for more of God
They say yes and we are still
Knowing a path-a way up
Following those who have witnessed the breath of God
Inspire us now one and all
To golden mean and peace across the land.

Unity is Real © 2020

Caught on a light breath
Carried to and through the wind
Inspiration bends.

Holy spirit fills
Peace comes knowing higher power
God's in action now.

Those who do not know
Bending all to their own will
Ignorance resists.

Unity persists
Those who bend, those who resist
Anchoring shared space.

Visions and dreams flow
Harmonize to golden mean
Unity is real.

The Warmth of Teachers' Ways © 2022

Your troubled heart now troubled mind
And body bares traumas left behind
In deepest reaches of your soul
You come to teachers to fill that hole.

And in the daily warp and woof
Of service to others is the proof
that pain and suffering can take hold
And turn body, mind, and spirit from warm to cold.

This frozen core is warmed again
Between teachers' hearts who are not some friends
They hold the space and enter in
To battle the demons you've framed as sins.

No fault or guilt or seeming shame
These teachers come with no need for gain
Ancient path of wisdom they seek to share
So the cold core will melt in the presence of care.

Defrosting begins when the student decides
To open their heart and no longer hide
Giving power to memories of hurts long ago
Instead catch new patterns now ready to sew.

The core of control to keep everything on ice
Facade of great knowing and so very "nice"
Dripping puddles now messy accepting the new
Teachers guiding the process - first one and then two.

The spirit now willing but still you resist
You like being frozen and start to insist
To teachers you summoned in humility one time
Now you say that your way, not their way, is ever sublime.

This core blocks true freedom of soul ever real
Decisions for change melt as the inner dweller would steal
A victory so near to find true nature encased
But you lose faith in teachers - turn on them your wrath

Glory be that their hearts are warmer than that
Your consent to be freed's their permission to bat
They then take a swing - seeing the pattern to go
Cold ice shattered - now melting - till you say the word "whoa."

A blessing to have teachers to your left and to your right
Core blockages' future is now out of sight
Standing ready a new person defined true nature so warm
For a while you may wonder if this process will harm.

The answer is "no" and you can trust what you've learned
Through this time of great melting your traumas have burned
Step forward in light - your new life begins today
Bless the teachers who stood beside you boldly and said
"it's our place" - "our way!"

A Mother's Hug © 2022

Seeking the only one who knows
We are the one she birthed and bathed
Our first memories she holds.

She is the one so perfect we know.
When our pain is great she cares
We seek the solace of her inviting arms.

She lives to be the best we all know
To hug the child born from her womb
Warmth felt in the embrace expressing her heart's beat.

Our mother's warm arms she does know
Absorbs us in the circle of heaven
Omega's touch coded for comfort and strength.

All through life this simple remedy we know
Kindness embodied in a mother's hug
She carries us in body, mind, and soul to starry bliss.